SHINE

39 tips for those winners who know that there is always room for improvement and who want to stand out from the crowd. Form better relationships, pick up ideas for generating money and feel more fulfilled as a human being.

BERNAT RIERA

DEDICATION

To my son

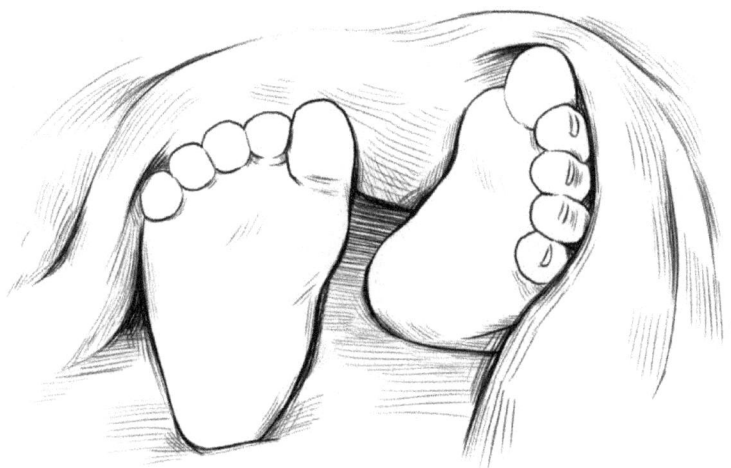

CONTENT

NO OTHER WAY THAN SUCCESS

You know what that means because we have seen winners in your work or in a friend, or because we ourselves have achieved great things in some facet of our life.

In this book, I want to encourage you to go from 'being good' to 'being standout'. To stand out from the rest. To inspire others, to leave the mediocre behind you and to follow your own path.

39 simple tips are provided for you to remember and to help you focus on what really matters, thus improving all facets of your life – not only on how to keep increasing your salary during your professional career or to invest wisely, but also in smaller details such as caring for your image, your diet or even taking care of projects that go beyond yourself, such as creating a company or leaving a legacy for your descendants.

Become more visible, shine with great achievements and learn to manage success.

The book is divided into four sections in which I intend you to: I) rise as an individual improving as a person and configure your mind properly; II) strengthen your relationships with others to make you feel happier; III) generate wealth in the medium and long-term with investment ideas and passive income generation habits; and IV) take your professional self as far as you can in your work with leadership and progression techniques.

Without a doubt, I know that you have all the desire and commitment to grow as a person and as a professional. How do I know?

Because you have this book in your hands and it is probably not the first or the last book of personal development that you have read. That's your advantage: knowing that even with you being good, you can be better, acquiring more knowledge, with more practice and with plenty of ambition. The mediocre are fine as they are – they do not even care. They are like those light bulbs that give little light and ignore the fact that with a thicker filament and with more energy they could shine more.

At the end of the book, you will have more confidence in yourself, with a new perspective on how to do things better and understand without jealousy why another winner is winning. I want you to not need to do a job interview again and to enjoy the greatest optimism of each precious stage of your life with your loved ones.

I.   SET UP YOUR BODY AND MIND FOR SUCCESS

1. AIM FOR THE GOLD AND FOR THE 'ALL'

Being hungry for success is a mentality and a way of life, and you have to be willing to give a lot and do a lot, to receive anything substantial. What is the difference between your life and those millionaires with houses near the beach, elite athletes, the "influencers" who charge for each publication in their social networks, artists or executives from large companies with strong political connections, capable of changing laws for the benefit of their business? Well, one day they decided to go for it and do whatever it took to get it.

Having the ambition to live better, be happier, generate more money, reach higher, or achieve great things for humanity is not a sin, but a virtue that many lack. In the end, those who have ambition are the only ones who will really get something beyond what they received at birth.

Forget that money does not buy happiness, or that big businessmen do not have time for their family ... First, money does not buy you happiness, but it will help you a lot when it comes to making decisions, like being able to pay for a better education or medical services for your children. And second, I do not want you to work 24 hours a day either, but you need to understand what will make you happy and go for it. Could it be that it is just having enough money, working one hour a day and being surrounded by the ones you love? Could be.

But with or without money, what you surely do not want is to work twelve hours a day, in a job that you didn't choose because you didn't have more options, where unfortunately, your bosses will not find it too difficult to find another capable to do your work, or even a machine!

The ambition to wish more will be your engine. It will be what makes you look up and what will push you to take one step after another. It will make you see that it is possible to rise to the next step towards success, leaving many others on the lower one.

With each new step, you will surround yourself with new friends and colleagues, and great talents that will help you to continue progressing in life. At each new level, you will have more power and more money that will lead you to generate more power and more money.

You go for the gold, for the greatness and for a better quality of life for you and for your loved ones. If, when you have already got the bronze, you think you do not want to go for more? That's okay, you always have time to relax and enjoy the success you have achieved to date, but aim to reach everything as a winner.

Are we still going?

2. DO WHATEVER IS IN YOUR HANDS TO BE HEALTHIER

Start with the most important – the foundation of anyone's well-being – your health.

You know that there are diseases and discomforts that we cannot anticipate, which can come from contagion, or from genetic causes or from simple, natural deterioration of the body, but here I will focus on preventing illness and improving your health as much as possible.

Start by paying attention to your body. Maybe it has been giving you signs that something is not as it should be: do you have frequent dizziness, are you always sneezing or coughing, have little energy, headaches, discomfort in a breast, or skin spots that don't disappear?

Consult with specialists and get regular checks today to reduce your visits to hospitals in the long term due to major problems. Sometimes we care more for the health of others than for our own, so try to take care of yourself as if someone had put you in charge of your own health – would you let yourself do everything you do?

In your day to day life, do not forget to watch your diet and exercise actively. The functioning of your body is comparable to a car: if you start to put bad gasoline and worse oil in, the internal parts will begin to wear out more quickly over time. Just like if the car is stopped for long periods, do not expect an excellent start or acceleration – but the more you use it properly, the better it will run overall.

Eating properly can be as simple as avoiding bad food. Find out about what each food category brings you and, balance and adjust your diet accordingly. It is not necessary to eat so much, nor always the same. I bet you already know that vegetables are better than Nutella.

The less processed the products you consume, the better they are for your body: fish, meat, eggs, rice, fruits and vegetables instead of packaged food products like cookies, pasta, bread or soft drinks such as cola.

Learn for yourself, because there are too many opinions. I have a strong breakfast with eggs, yoghurt and fruit to start the day with high energy, leaving my lighter intake for dinner, helping me to rest better and not have to digest food while I sleep.

Exercise routinely, whether it's taking walks, going to the gym, swimming or doing yoga. Depending on your age and the physical capacity you have, your level of demand will vary.

Physical activity causes your heart to pump at different pulse rates and keeps your organs and muscles active, creating a sense of inner well-being.

Remember that you only have one body and that you should keep it in the best possible state for many years.

Think of it in the long term.

3. SLEEP AND RESET YOUR BODY AND MIND

To get a good rest is as important to your health as your diet and physical exercise, and causes a complete reboot of your system every night, just as you were programmed.

The human mind and body are such a complex machine that we will never fully understand how it all works. One thing we do know – one of our main "limitations" to stop us from continuing working at the highest level, in addition to food and movement, is that we need to rest.

Sleep resets the body and mind and allows you to be optimal the next day. A bad rest, on the other hand, will cause you anxiety, lack of control, and will prevent you from enjoying your days, dramatically deteriorating your professional and personal results.

Everybody prefers different conditions to rest as well as possible, according to their health, lifestyle or the stage they are at in their life: being a child, parent, hi-stress employee, physical worker, etc. You likely know your preferred conditions at all times. Some of us need six hours, while others need eight, plus a power nap in the afternoon. Some need conditions of absolute silence and darkness and others can sleep happily, regardless of their environment.

Our generation is fortunate in being able to analyze our personal sleep habits. There are apps, wristbands and other wearables that allow you to monitor your rest every night and depending on how you move or breathe, you can know the depth that you rested and you can evaluate how that quality affected your next day's performance. When you discover that eating late, eating too much, drinking alcohol or caffeine, watching TV, or even the type of pillow you have makes your sleep worse, you can discover and correct this and instantly start having a better quality of life. For example, I use the app 'Sleep Cycle' (one of many), with which, after monitoring my nights for more than two years, I can see how, on those evenings I ate fish for dinner, I slept 5% better than the average of all my nights, or how my sleeping fared on that day it rained (+ 3%), when I had a stressful work day (-12%), if I went swimming (+6%), if those nights were a full moon (+ 8%) or if the next day I had important meetings or presentations (-3%).

When you discover what conditions affect your sleep, you can correct them and have a better quality of life. When I have a hard day at work, I try to go for a swim, or eat fish, to help me relax, disconnect and rest better.

An additional tip: if you are someone who uses your mobile or computer before going to bed, put them in night mode, which eliminates the blue tones of the screen, creating a more yellow, warm and relaxing light for the eyes and brain. Mobiles such as iPhone or Android have it by default and, for the computer, I use 'F.lux', which gradually reduces the brightness and blue colour during the evening.

Happy dreams - Best days.

4. ONLY WORRY ABOUT WHAT'S IN YOUR CONTROL

Well, you are feeling healthier, stronger, revitalized and with a lot of energy to face the harder days. But what about the days when the events overwhelm you, you have a lot of work, your new-born daughter cries non-stop or your bosses do not understand you? Having worries is part of life and you should separate them in two categories: those you can control and those you cannot.

For things that are out of your control, you will have to learn not to worry – seriously. There is too much chaos in the middle of order. And those that are controllable, learn to evaluate them and to make better decisions.

I'll start with the first category, with a simple and rational question:

Why worry about something that you cannot do anything to avoid or to solve? It will only create distress and anguish, and the results will happen in any case, whatever it may be, and without your influence. If you've missed a plane by being late, if your partner has broken up with you for another person or if the competition got that big contract. It hurts, but the only thing you have to think about is how you will react to different scenarios or events, and once you have your response to those problems ready and under control, then you will feel much more relieved: buy another flight, reinvent yourself and improve to meet a new great person, or analyze what made that competitor better and what new value you could create so that the next customer will choose your company without even comparing you to others.

But wait a minute... are you sure you cannot do anything to change the future result? Maybe it's not too late to wake up early enough to prevent a possible traffic jam that will take you to the airport next week? Not too late to hire young people for your company who will innovate to be more competitive?

It's in your hands to become an indispensable employee for your company today and not end up being one of the heads that roll in tomorrow's budget cuts. If it's already tomorrow, and layoffs are imminent, work on a plan of reaction for after being fired, like starting to think about other companies in which you could have good opportunities, or about undertaking that business you always wanted to try, or about travelling for a few months around the world to decide the next big step in your professional career will be.

Finally, remember that the way someone else is or behaves is also out of your control, so you can worry and care about them, inevitably, because of your empathy, but you won't change them. Those loved ones or colleagues at work who don't act as you would, they will disappoint and worry you, but their futures depend on themselves, not on you. Sometimes, the only thing we can do is advise and then to sit back, accepting that we all have a brain with which we think rationally and make decisions, and it's not your job to think for everyone.

5. MAKE DECISIONS TODAY THINKING IN 10 YEARS

There are concerns in your life that are under your control and over which you will have to make many decisions every day to prevent future problems which, fortunately, are in your hands. For many, evaluating and making decisions, however small or large, can create anxiety. But you are going to have the key to making big decisions: think about the long term.

It is normal that you make decisions today, remembering how you felt in the past, either with that person, with previous experiences in which you learned something or, conversely, where you did not have any experience about that issue and where now you are afraid to decide. For instance, you do not want to leave that job that is being a nightmare for you because your friends took a long time to find a new job after resigning and even some of them regret moving, or are still unemployed. But you have to be brave and make important decisions today to improve your quality of life 10 years from now, and that could mean quitting that job as soon as possible and looking for something in which you spend your hours happily.

The experiences or shortcomings of the past can help us to create an opinion or feeling, but they should not set the tone for how we plan our bright future.

On the other hand, there are also those who have had a worse experience and therefore make decisions based on the present situation and how they feel today about it. These decisions are more emotional, and I consider them more as reactions to an imminent situation than thoughtful decisions, and are equally risky or ill-advised. This may include buying an excellent sports car even though you have nothing saved to pay for your studies. Or like being unfaithful based on an irrational, short-term decision about obtaining pleasure in the moment.

How will my decision today affect my future quality of life, or the people around me? How irreversible is this decision, and what risk does it entail?

Some paths (or decisions) seem easier to take than others, faster, less crooked, or less steep. But thinking about the long term, you will realize that other, more challenging roads will take you to the summit you want to reach.

6. THE VISUAL IMAGE OF ONESELF

You feel good, you go for it all and you have a new body and mind configuration that will allow you to go further than ever. This means you should also be seen as a winner.

There are exceptions of course, but winners tend to make those around them feel comfortable in their presence, and people want to talk to them, be seen with them, and be part of their circle.

Do they look good because they are winners, or was looking good part of their winning formula? I would bet on the latter.

The impression we make on others, whether we like it or not, is judged by the visual impact we cause and the perception of that look in those who observe it. And even though that perception can change across different people, beauty standards are quite universal.

Imagine this: it's midnight, you're alone in the street walking, when suddenly, you hear someone approaching behind you. You subtly turn to see who it is, and you see a person dressed in sports clothes and a cap hiding his face. Closer and closer. Do you feel as safe as if the person approaching were wearing a suit and tie? It may literally be the same person, but our perception changes.

Dress with style and class according to your industry, or people with whom you have relationships, but always make sure that your clothes are clean every day no matter what, and your shoes are not the same ones you have worn for four years. Save on drinks, not on quality clothes or accessories such as watches or umbrellas.

When you talk to people, keep a smile on your face most of the time to transmit that inner happiness and the fact that you are happy to be talking to them. If you do not have a good smile, get it now with your dentist, not only for the health of your teeth, but for their aesthetic. Orthodontics and teeth whitening can raise your confidence to levels you never imagined.

Go to image professionals, make-up artists, and hairdressers, and ask them what could work best with your physical type. Do not take for granted that you already have the best hair colour, style of clothing, or the makeup that best suits you. Even if you do, you should at least dare to reinvent yourself from time to time.

Know your physiognomy and learn how to get the best out of it, such as your height, the colour of your eyes, hair or facial features, among other things.

Invest in an elegant car and keep it clean, so that you are not ashamed if you pick someone up unexpectedly.

Invest in a house and keep it clean, well lit, with plants, spacious and orderly, in which any guest feels comfortable.

7. SILENCE THE NOISE THAT SURROUNDS YOU AND REFOCUS

To shine, you will have to constantly strive, work hard and dedicate many hours of your free time. We live in an ultra-connected society, with our phones and computers in constant conversation with one another. We're bombarded by all that information in the digital world, in our pockets, from TV and even in the street, on advertising posters. There is a lot of noise, and filtering between what is valuable and not is an art.

You are preparing yourself to endure more stressful situations than most people live in and, for this reason, it is important that you also know how to relax and know how to stop from time to time, to come back stronger.

Save some time for yourself to disconnect; avoid distractions and enjoy silence and solitude for a moment. Let all the snowflakes in this crystal ball rest on the bottom again, and allow yourself to see what really matters with greater clarity, which may be a goal or a person or a project you've started.

Everyone needs to learn their own best way to disconnect which will allow them to restructure their thoughts. Maybe you can relax and refocus during a hike in the mountains among nature. You may sail at sunrise or sit on the sand watching the sunset. Educate yourself to associate that moment and place of your disconnection, so as soon as you take the time to go there, your brain will enter a relaxing mode and see things with better perspective.

Avoid alcohol because, although you think it relaxes you and helps you to disconnect, you will not be completely lucid to refocus on your future or to be as productive when you return to work.

Disconnect in a different place other than where you spend most of your time – like your dining room or bedroom – but somewhere a little more special. Somewhere where it's you, you with yourself. You can be sitting in a quiet spot in a local park, in the sauna, or going for a run, among other environments and situations, but you cannot be listening to people or reading. That way, you will get information out of your brain, instead of introducing more.

Some of the most important decisions in my professional career were made while tapping a ball about in a London park.

8. UNDERSTAND WHY YOU EXIST

The last personal pillar that you must configure in your mind is about the value that you will leave beyond your own existence, to understand why everything makes sense.

Humans have many centuries of history and our ancestors lived for the same number of years (or even fewer) than you, so in the end, your time here is relatively short and you will disappear with the big question: Have I contributed with anything to the human species so that the following generations can evolve with it?

Most people do not care about that, but you want to consciously contribute something more than your footsteps and, in order to be remembered in your absence, you must achieve great things in this life, always pursuing a goal much greater than yourself.

So, the great mission we all have is to help the evolution of humanity. And having fun as much as possible while we do it!

There are many people who have achieved very important things during their life and because of them, we are where we are today. Great inventors like Edison, thanks to whom today's energy can be distributed to each house, companies like NASA, who explore space, geniuses like Tim Berners-Lee, who created the World Wide Web and made it accessible to everyone, Steve Jobs with the iPhone or Elon Musk creating multiple companies that intend to change the world, such as Tesla, SpaceX or OpenAI, among thousands of other individuals who have dedicated their lives to a cause greater than their own time of life.

And I'm not talking about personal achievements such as getting a career, keeping the house clean, spending your day working in someone else's company, spending your evenings in the pub, and still feeling fulfilled.

But to participate in the construction of a new hospital in Congo, to develop a new online application used by thousands of people, to plant trees in a deforested area, to work in politics and have power to change some laws for the benefit of citizens and their prosperity, or even to educate your own child conscientiously by being an exemplary mother or father.

These previous paragraphs shouldn't leave you indifferent: either they bothered you because I am telling you that the hours you spend watching TV do not help the world to progress, or you were thinking that there is so much to be done and you will die trying.

The latter ones, please welcome to the next level.

9. SET ANNUAL GOALS

And what better than to go step by step, year by year, growing as a person, contributing to the world and generating your wealth bit by bit.

To do this, you will set annual goals with which you will keep the focus on what and where to invest your time and money to be able to continue progressing.

These goals have to be realistic, feasible to be achieved in this time frame and they need to depend on you, because, if you do not achieve them, it must be your own fault for not making the effort and without excuses.

Write them on a large blackboard in your room or similar format where you see them each morning upon awakening and each night when you go to sleep, adding a mark or bar on each of the goals you worked on that day to achieve. It can be a small step, like a call, or a very big and definitive one, like the signing of a corporate acquisition. Each step counts towards achieving your goal and you will give the same importance to every effort. The motivation is to move forward, however, every day.

Set several and diverse goals around your persona so, by the end of the year, you have improved many aspects of it; like becoming a better wife or husband, mother or father, employee, leader, or to improve your physique, make new or better friends, obtain more purchasing power, more customers or fewer expenses.

'Getting fit' is not a good goal because it is difficult to measure and you will not know when you achieved it. Instead, define the kilos of weight or millimetres of fat you want to reduce by the end of the year, or the meters per minute that you are able to run, the number of Olympic pool lengths you can swim, or the number of repetitions you are able to do of a specific exercise. So, every day that you do something towards that goal, mark it, like when you refuse to drink alcohol at a party or eat certain unhealthy foods, every time you go to train or even if you walked to work instead of using the car.

Other examples of tangible goals could be: to be able to have a phone conversation with a foreigner in another language, to dedicate at least 15% of your hours to your partner, to win a pool tournament, to reduce your household expenses by half comparing December with January of the same year, to finish a master's degree, to make at least three trips out of the country, to write a children's book or to increase your income per hour worked, among many others.

At the end of the year, in addition to seeing how you ended the year with more value than you started and knowing that you can achieve anything you invest effort in, you will see that the goals that you didn't achieve are those with fewer marks or daily efforts.

II.   BE EXCELLENT WITH OTHERS

10. STRENGTHEN YOUR RELATIONS

In this section, you will learn to be more aware of how your relationships work and how to improve your interactions with others, since, according to research studies in human psychology, relationships with others are the main cause of your happiness; to belong to a social community, to a family, to have friends and emotional relationships.

You are programmed to interact with others, to love and receive love, at whatever level. So, don't be too lazy about socializing in events, spending time with your partner or stay out with your usual friends, who continue to meet regularly as if they had nothing else to do.

To keep close to your friends may require to leave your ego at home – ego is the best friend of loneliness. We all like to be called, to be felt interested, to be offered plans, but the reality is that nobody picks up the phone.

So, take the phone, go to Whatsapp and go down through the list of messages to see who you have not contacted for some time and take the initiative.

Sign up for social activities in groups such as IT geeks, reading clubs, cooking classes, a basketball team or any other activity that allows you to interact with others, where you will get to know them more and more over time.

As in everything, you want to have a balance – I'm not saying that you should spend all day in a cafe or in the company kitchen talking. After all, don't forget that it is just as important to dedicate some time to your success and to your performance as it is to establish strong social bonds.

And if you have opted for marriage with a person to whom you have committed, then dedicate time, love and much respect.

Do not take the relationship for granted and invest dedication and effort. Remember how you talked to him or her when you started dating, how you spent your time together and the wonderful times you had with each other. If that is changing, you should take action before it is too late, and if you no longer feel the same, then talk to your partner but do not cheat. Leave aside the sexual desire of wanting to be with another person, since the desire is just that: desire. Can you imagine wishing something that you already have?

Strive to become more connected with others. Love and offer your help no matter whether they do the same. You know how to earn things – and now, also people.

11. BE POLITE AND RESPECTFUL

You want to shine as a person, you want to be loved, to please and get far in business and in your life in general. And you know what? Nobody has achieved that by being rude or disrespectful to others.

If you intend to be outstanding with others, start by laying a good foundation, and show manners and class first.

Open the door so people can get in or leave before you, when you both meet in a doorway. Allowing yourself to lose two seconds can strongly impact how others perceive you.

Let pregnant women and people with difficulties, who are standing on public transport, sit down. Or ask other passengers to let them sit down if either they haven't noticed it for themselves or the people who need it don't ask for it.

Serve water and wine to the people sitting at the table and ensure you are the last to be served. Look at the person speaking to you, pay attention and demonstrate interest with affirmations or questions.

Be the first to take out your wallet when paying and leave a tip on the table, even if no one else does. You are not the fool of the group for being the only one who leaves a tip – rather, you are the only one who is considerate, grateful and generous.

Respect other drivers, give way to cars that are turning into your lane or pedestrians crossing and keep alert with cyclists and motorcyclists around you.

Talk to the person who is being set apart in a conversation. Force others to open the circle and include that person.

Help to cook, clean, go shopping and other everyday tasks that you share with your partner. Ask someone how you can help them and offer a bit of your time or money.

Stop interrupting people when they speak. Be quiet. Allow time for everyone to participate in the conversation, and learn to listen more. I already warn you that it will be frustrating for you to patiently wait your turn with respect and let the rest speak, especially if when you start talking, another interrupts you, but this is the difference between the two. If you really want to be heard, you can say with a friendly tone: "Can we apply the two-minute rule, in which we take turns and each one of us has two minutes to share their opinion without interruptions?"

Although many things are common sense and were taught to us as children, you will be surprised to see how many people are not aware of their selfish or inconsiderate behaviour.

And, unfortunately, they are so common that by practising the above, you will start to get attention from the people around you.

12. BE THERE

I see them in meetings, on the phone, when they are having dinner at home, when they walk with their children in the park, or even, I guess, when they are making love with their partner. They are elsewhere.

You are going to stand out from the rest with a very simple action: put your mind and all your senses in the same place as your body, and if your mind is in another place, start moving your body towards it.

Enjoy time with your daughter while you are with her. Play with her, show her new things, hug her and make her laugh, not resorting to devices or screen tactics. And don't worry, the emails will still be in your inbox in a couple of hours.

Really taste the food of a restaurant and talk with the person who is with you. Or spend time to prepare a nice and elaborate dinner from time to time.

Add value to the meeting you attend and set your laptop and emails aside. Ask and give your opinion.

Average people are everywhere, and doing everything. The best, though, are interested – they feel, they comment, they laugh, they support, they celebrate, they discuss, they focus and they progress when they do all this.

Then there are also those who are attentive and present, but only during that given moment in time, and forget after a while. Differentiate yourself from them by following up on what's going on around them after a while; ask how their child did in that exam which they probably weren't expecting you to ask about.

Send an email listing the actions after that meeting or next steps after that call with the boss and investors.

Ask about that medical test.

Buy her that perfume that she was testing at the airport and she kept smelling on her wrist.

Write down all these observations in your favourite notebook, review it every week and start becoming outstanding among your friends. From now on, you will have a different vision for things by capturing all these details.

The more present you are in each moment of your day, the happier you will be appreciating the things and people around you and the more productive you will be, by focusing well on each task that concerns you.

13. HELP THOSE YOU CAN

Not because of karma, or because they ask you to. Help as much as you can for the simple reason that you can do it. You have the capacity, resources and time that many in the most unfavourable situations lack.

We see people in need at all times throughout the day: in the news, in adverts from NGOs, or in our social networks. And, as well as empathizing with these difficulties, due to our ability to perceive and understand, it creates a sense of impotence and frustration to think that we cannot stop that war in Syria, or the diseases or malnutrition that affect so many children in African towns, or the incomprehensible, yet demonstrable corruption in first world countries.

But, still, there are many people that you can help. They are much closer to you and you have the possibility to improve their lives.

You can share your knowledge. You are educated, you read much more than most and you have mastered certain topics, so it is most likely that there are occasions when you can give some advice to people about something they are thinking of doing.

Help people with needs in your own neighbourhood or city, such as homeless. Do not stereotype them, since each is in that situation for a different reason; some are overcoming an addiction, others received a good education but have had bad luck, while some suffer from mental illness, etc. These people feel absolutely alone and that destroys any human being. You can help them with just a conversation, a greeting, or by showing some interest in their history. Instead of giving them coins, take some gift cards with which they can buy food in stores or restaurants, and can get off the street for a while. Energy bars or bottles of water that fit easily in your bag could be of great help.

Look for initiatives in your city that need volunteers and offer a day of your month to help. Your help could be needed by an organization that wants to clean the beaches or forests, as well as by a friend who needs to move furniture from their old house to their new one.

Check out the job offers relevant for you and don't completely ignore those not relevant for your profile, because they could be a great opportunity for your friends or family. Tell them about that opportunity which could mean the next step for their professional careers.

If you are a pianist, you could play for an afternoon in a nursing home and get their eyes off the TV for a pleasant time.

If you are a masseuse, you will find many people exhausted in hospitals from having spent the night awake, or with high accumulated tension.

There is plenty to be done in the world, and each of us has the capacity to help.

14. FAMILY RELATIONSHIPS

Having good family relationships will be very important when it comes to having a solid and stabilized base. Normally, we take for granted these connections, which we do not necessarily work to nurture or sustain, setting this aside for pre-established dates such as Christmas or very specific events.

Do you remember that relative who got sick, and even though he had a lot of friends, the visitors in the hospital were basically family? Some friends visited during the first few days, but after weeks or months, he only received visits from close relatives, who even rotated to spend the night in uncomfortable chairs.

Your family is the only thing you are born with and the only thing you can count on unconditionally being stuck with throughout your life, and you could not even choose it, so it is normal to have better relationships with some than with others. But do not avoid those who have seen you grow up, like your brothers, cousins, uncles, parents or grandparents, as well as new members who have been incorporated over the years, like wives, husbands and children.

You know that it is not easy for a family to be strong and united among all its connections, and you are possibly even now thinking about some members of the family who are harder to get on with because of various conflicts. I get it – each situation is different of course – but a common factor in family problems is money concerns, so I want you to change this today, for the benefit of the next generation, because you have understood the importance of generating money and giving it away, instead of spending and asking for it. Avoid clashes over inheritances by asking your members to leave their legacies in order as soon as possible. Organize family meals and invite them. Give them gifts frequently and with meaning.

Don't worry if some think that they are taking advantage of your generosity. What you are doing is educating your children and theirs about how things should be done in this family, so they will also do it with their future children. Dynamics change.

Break traditions and show them that you care and not only on specific dates. Invite your aunt to come home to eat on a Sunday with her husband and children, if she has them, although it would also be convenient to give her the opportunity to meet you alone sometimes, in case she needs that confidentiality to tell you something a little more personal or express herself with more freedom. Offer yourself and support her when you have the opportunity, and make that relationship stronger.

Visit your mother any day she is not expecting it, and let her know first thing in the morning. In this way, you will make her happy not only during your visit, but during the entire wait.

If you have the opportunity, connect with a new layer of your family connections, such as your partner's family, and the families of their partners. Maybe you are two links away to meeting your best future partner or a new great friend.

Expand your family, and forge relationships.

15. BUSINESS WITH FAMILY OR FRIENDS

You want all three: a big united family, lots of real friends and a great business, but be careful when mixing the ingredients.

A family business may have been running for some time prior to you arriving on the scene, and you must adapt to the system already in place, in the interests of learning about it and improving it during your time, with a view to passing it to your descendants as happened with you.

It will be difficult to have the same bosses both at work and at home, but if you respect each other, set limits and separate work from your family relationships, there should be no problem.

If, on the other hand, instead of inheriting a business legacy you are starting a new business venture with a friend or a relative, be very careful with clarity of roles and responsibilities, or you could put at risk what unites you.

Businesses that work with friends tend to best work when each person brings something very defined and different from one another – such as bringing a specific skill, providing capital investment, the number of hours they are able to work – and each role is vital and distinct, such as management, technical skills, sales expertise, and customer relations, among other responsibilities.

Entrepreneurship involves a big economic effort and involvement to make any headway in any market, so define the role of each of you in the company. Ensure it is crystal clear and set down in writing.

Agree on reviewing everyone's performance in some way every

certain period of time, so if anyone isn't pulling their weight, that person can be made to realize this themselves.

The more partners and friends there are in the equation, the more delicate that structure will be in terms of what's needed to preserve the friendship. If you are more than two, it will be better that you all agree who will be in charge, since otherwise you could be blocked in every decision that should be taken, and paralysed by having too many opinions and decision makers.

So, don't try to get involved in any idea that a friend proposes after having a few drinks. Nor should you try to seduce them with a project you have in mind for which you think you need a partner, only because the investment is too high for you.

Evaluate what you really need and define the qualities of that partner appropriately – there are many Internet portals where you can request services from freelancers (who work on their own, on single projects) and you can adapt your resources to the needs that arise without high costs – not having to make commitments with relatives or friends.

16. MEET NEW PEOPLE

It's great that you have and keep all these groups of friends who have been there for a long time, but it's also important, and more challenging, to know how to expand that circle for both your own social welfare and for those important professional connections, which is known as networking.

Start with the simplest: your friends and current connections are an inexhaustible source of potential new relationships, which they could be introduced to during a game of tennis or having a few beers.

Connecting with someone's friend is starting the relationship from a much more advanced position already based on trust, rather than from scratch.

You also have to prepare yourself to establish totally new relationships with unknown people, either through social events, work or other occasions, in which you will have the opportunity to establish a first contact.

Be smart and analyse the context to see if it would be a good idea to talk to them. If so, look for a safe and friendly, disinterested approach and handle it with great care. This is because many put themselves in a defensive position when someone unknown comes to talk to them, especially if they are concerned there is any sexual interest.

Start talking about your common ground – being in that place, time, and with other people in common is not merely a coincidence. Try to understand as quickly as possible whether having that person in your closest circle of connections is in your interests: Is there any business opportunity, common hobby, or other personal interest for you or someone else you know?

If yes, then move on to the next stage: Understand how you can help them. That's right – to receive, first you have to give, and you have to know what they need, want or what keeps them up at night.

If you do not know, ask them directly: "Hey, is there anything you need help with? I know enough people that if I or they can help you with anything." Their surprise is guaranteed, and probably they will lower their guard and disclose more information about themselves: "Well, do you know somebody who knows about watches?" or "Who would like to invest in a new business venture?".

Manage that information to establish a new, mutually beneficial and long-term relationship. Help them yourself or connect them with others. Soon, the results will come back to you.

Meeting people will open up new opportunities and shorten many paths.

17. DEVELOP YOUR SOCIAL INTELLIGENCE

Your sociability and relationship with others is a strategy game involving everyone else' personalities and interests, which you must use to learn how to identify them. And the advantage is that others don't know they are being analysed while you are deciding how to act and/or trying to manipulate the situation for your benefit.

There are several factors that impact how another person perceives you, such as the chemistry between the two of you, the character of each of you, plus the personal circumstances at a given time. Therefore, you have to gather as much information as you can, before a joke could offend the other party and break a deal, or you fight with your child without taking into account the difficulties he's having at school which he hides to avoid further reprisals. Before speaking, make sure you completely know the listener and adjust your message, tone, and how to transmit it to him or her.

Many people will be more introverted than you and for them to socialize will feel awkward and unpleasant. Help them, and always be the one who approaches them without feeling bad about it. Introduce them to other groups of friends and become a key person in their circles.

If, on the other hand, you consider yourself the introvert, try to regularly leave your comfort zone and lead the conversations and relationships or, smartly, influence those who like to be leading those social groups.

You can close some important business deals with a good supplier or customer by making a quick call and getting to the point, although with others you may have to go for lunch and talk about other issues for hours. Analyse the conversation constantly and let it deviate if it comes naturally, but bring it back again when you have the chance.

You will motivate certain people by congratulating them for any little thing they do and, for others, although having great achievements, you may have to push them by telling them that it is not enough and that they can achieve much more next time.

Identify the personality of each one, since each person in front of you is different and there is no exact formula.

And, if you have doubts about how to act, do not hurry. Instead, listen more and do not talk so much, or assume that they are the ones analysing you – and in that case, take good care of your words!

18. TRAVEL AND SEE THE WORLD

Everything revolves around you and your relationships with others, no matter where they are from. Travelling will allow you to discover beautiful scenarios and meet valuable people, in addition to returning more rested and full of new ideas.

The day-to-day lives of people from different locations around the world are different: cultures, the colour of the ocean, the greens of the mountains and trees, the waterfalls, their cities and small towns, their animals and their understanding of life.

You cannot know and see everything, but at least you can try to enjoy this precious gift of life to its fullest.

Learn something new on each trip and leave some value for the people you have come across. Ask them a lot and explain to them a lot more in return, if they show interest. To have a good level of English would be very helpful, because if you don't speak the same language, English will be the best chance of you both understanding each other.

Beyond people, visit the historical legacies of their society, intimate corners, impossible landscapes, spectacular buildings, and typical restaurants or bars, to ensure you have a range of different experiences. Understand the history and context of all these places to appreciate the why, how, and when of each place's existence.

The evolution of the Internet and transport have both flattened the world, and any city is accessible to most of us at an affordable price. Intercontinental flights are relatively low-cost, and search engines like skyscanner.com allow you to find combinations of destinations and dates to get the best offer, if you are somewhat flexible.

With booking.com or airbnb.com you can find houses from any local area becoming your private home and you can have a much more local experience than a large hotel chain will give you.

Thanks to smartphones with Internet and GPS, you can locate and safely navigate the streets of any country with digital maps, find points of interest, shops, restaurants and discover the best routes using public transport to reach your desired destination.

If you are curious but you can't physically fly, remember that with the Internet you can learn about any country, as well as being able to virtually visit any place thanks to the wealth of virtual reality and even establish contact with locals via Facebook or an international forum about a common hobby.

The privileges we have today for visiting the world mean you have no excuses and should push you to step out of your local bubble. Privileges that our previous generations never dreamed of.

19. LEAVE A LEGACY TO THOSE WHO FOLLOW YOU

Because in this section I intend you to get closer to other people, there are no stronger ties than the ones you have with family members and, above all, if you have them, with your descendants.

You have the opportunity to achieve great things during your life, whether or not you have inherited opportunities from your family. From here and now, it's all on you, and when you are not here anymore, your children or relatives will continue with your story and legacy.

Try to invest or strive for projects that go beyond your lifetime and make it easier for those who come after, so they can devote themselves to and invest in new projects built on top of your contribution to the world.

Buying land or property is a great long-term investment in which you can rarely lose out, and is one of the best legacies you can leave to your successors.

When these properties belong to your descendants, they will have increased their value considerably and you will be facilitating either a place for the next generation to live (and save costs) or a reliable stream of income through renting, or sale if necessary.

Creating a brand or company can be invaluable as long as your organisation's economic prospects make sense and your successors inherit a business model that generates money and employment, and not debts or headaches.

So, if you felt imprisoned in your own company, and you do not see its prospects improving when your children take over, it might be better to liquidate it or sell it and simply pay for them to have the best possible education.

Beyond a physical legacy, you could also transmit your knowledge, writings or teachings about a subject that your children will be unlikely to learn in school – for instance, investing wisely their money or treating older people with respect.

Take them to the best local college you can afford, because besides betting on who can have the best educational system and the most committed teachers in their success and development, you will be surrounding your kids with other children who are also receiving a high level of education and support, who in the future, may be well positioned in their careers and be able to give great advice to their friends.

Help them to improve their level of English. Invite them to live abroad and to aspire to go to the best international colleges and universities.

The sooner you understand your time here is short, but that you are still an important link in your family's chain, the bigger and greater will be the projects you will be inspired to get involved in.

III.   INCREASE YOUR PERSONAL WEALTH DAY BY DAY

20. HUNGER OF KNOWLEDGE

It's said that when you stop learning, you start to die.

I have met many who think they are very good at something and have laughed at the possibility of learning more, especially if it is something they think they have mastered. They are their own barrier and, honestly, do not worry about them, because they will never compete with you.

No matter your age, experience, skills or abilities, remember there is never a time when a person cannot increase their personal visibility through continuous learning. Our value is created by our knowledge and how we apply it in any aspect of our life. You have to keep learning to extend that brightness over time and not to make it something finite.

You already know at what pace technology advances and that any of us could have a job disappear because of evolution – a new software or machine that can do it at a lower cost, a new app that will revolutionize the market as Uber or Airbnb did, a new intern in the company full of energy and new ideas, or even a change in customer demand that lowers the price of an asset that you sell. So it is vital to stay competitive and versatile to adapt to what your professional future holds.

Help a chef to cook, and learn. Then, ask them to look at you and guide you while you cook. In the future, repeat with a different chef.

Ask the intern for help to observe his new technique of doing something that you already knew and repeat him without fear until you have perfected it.

Read blogs and books, watch videos on YouTube, listen to audiobooks while driving, walking or being in the gym (I use Amazon's Audible platform which has a huge library).

Help others to do their work and learn during the process.

There are many online platforms you can use: Udemy, Lynda, Coursea and YouTube, as well as offline, libraries full of resources or the brains of your own friends.

Ask, seek and absorb knowledge continuously and do not let the new technological wave pass over you.

At the time I am writing this book, smartphones, 3D printers, virtual reality, nanotechnology, the Internet of things, rockets that reach Mars and artificial intelligence have been invented. Consequently, the following generations will be born with all of that from their first day and will be the ones really finding a use for them that we cannot even imagine, in addition to everything they will invent during their own time.

21. EVERY HOUR OF YOUR DAY HAS TO GENERATE MORE

It's great to have a job that you like, where you feel valued in the company and even have a good salary, but that will not get you rich.

So, the first concept that you have to be clear about, if you want to amass a fortune, is that you should not be exchanging the hours of your day for a salary, since, however much they pay you, your time is limited and you cannot increase your income exponentially.

You have to generate more money for each hour worked, as well as for those where you don't work but rest. Imagine getting up in the morning and having been generating a small fortune while you were sleeping. You will achieve this by creating one or more systems that generate income passively, on which you spend very little time and produce a return.

How do you do it? First of all, having a thorough control of all your money inflows and all the hours you work to produce them. That's your profitability per hour worked out, and you need to increase it every year.

Secondly, invest time or money in something that allows you to generate income over a long period of time. Here are some ideas of passive income:

Buy properties and rent them: on a holiday basis, for long-term tenants, per room for students or any other configuration.

Create an online store (Ecommerce) in which users can buy products at any time and from anywhere. When you have a good product, create an online store with Shopify very easily.

Create and sell content such as writing, videos, blogs, photos, music ... and distribute it across your audience for a fee. This is content that, once created, can be sold indefinitely without needing additional effort.

Use Amazon to buy and sell products between countries or from different suppliers, getting a profit margin per transaction. Or you can also use other alternatives to Amazon, like eBay, or Etsy.

On the other hand, if you are already a successful entrepreneur in a business, you will know that once you have created a new company and it works, you have to create a system that replaces you. Therefore, make sure the company doesn't need you actively and you can dedicate your time to another thing or even to creating the next company, but don't let the success and special affection you have for a company you created enslave you from sunrise to sunset.

There are many different ideas, but get the drip of income to increase every month: this is your cashflow. Get more for less, and start devoting your free time to the things that give you more happiness.

22. INVEST, OR SAVE TO INVEST

Once we generate more income per month, we will have to know what to do with the money. It'll be a sweet problem, and the sweet solution is to put it back in, to generate even more.

It's easy to think that you could spend it and enjoy a better quality of life, but it will also be important that you save a part of your salary and invest another part each month.

Separate at least ten percent of your total income into a different bank account that allows you to accumulate enough cash you might need one day for an emergency, for your retirement, for a big trip, for the purchase of a car or even to be reinvested, like for the initial payment of a house.

Another percentage of your income has to be invested to generate more. You want to put your money to work for you, instead of you working for it.

As I wrote above, buying land, a house or apartment means a very safe long-term investment and you can convert it into liquidity at any time you need it through sale or rent.

There are many other investments that you can make with smaller amounts or without getting into debt with a bank, like buying artwork (paintings, sculptures), jewellery (diamonds, gold), and any other piece in a collection that increases its value over time due to its shortage of production and high demand.

You can also invest in the stock market, although this assumes a bit more risk. You could buy shares from a strong and stable company that pays dividends every quarter regardless of the fluctuation of its stock, although you will have to invest large amounts so that the profits are notable.

You can also buy shares of companies where you think their stock price is going to go up over time because the fundamentals of the company are very strong and will allow you to sell them at a higher value than you bought them after a few months or years. And calm down if the shares you own begin to fall in value. Do not worry unnecessarily and, of course, avoid selling low. There are hundreds or thousands of workers in that company working hard to raise its value. Wait, and if you want to sell, sell them when they are up again.

If you like to invest in companies but don't want to put all your eggs in one basket, you can diversify your portfolio by investing in indices that agglomerate the results of the best companies in Spain (IBEX35 – the best 35) or the USA (S&P500 – its best 500), among other markets. And do you know what happens when a company stops performing well and falls out of the list of the 35 best public companies in Spain? That one leaves and another high performer enters. It sounds pretty sure to me.

To start investing in companies or indexes, you can talk to your bank or register with any online trader like deGiro, eToro or Plus500.

23. PRODUCE AND STOP CONSUMING

You are born as a consumer.

It's what you have always seen through people around you, and what you have always been educated with. You read books, buy gadgets, eat in restaurants, drive a nice car and entertain yourself in bars or cinemas.

But from now on, you, as a successful person, are going to change your lenses and the way you see the world. Glory is on the other side, with those who produce what others consume.

When you go to Amazon to buy, stop for a second and think about what you could be selling on that platform instead. When you read this book, realize that you could also write yours. Develop a new website that finally covers the needs of people like you that are searching the Internet.

Once you break that mental barrier and believe that you can produce instead of consume, you will start to see opportunities everywhere: for example, there are those people playing with apps on their mobiles that you could be developing (or paying developers to do it), or instead of eating with your partner in that restaurant which has interesting concepts, you could try to copy and improve, or change the ingredients.

Develop ideas that could apply to a different social class (you know that some are willing to pay more than others for the same product or service), for different languages (that successful idea is currently working in England but does not exist in France yet) or for different cultures (a type of foreign cuisine that could create a trend in your city).

And not only that, think big! Once, someone like you decided to manufacture a new automobile brand although there were already others in the market.

Someone else put together a script, which took actors, a director and some investment to create that movie you have watched twice.

Buy in one country and sell in others, making a margin.

Ask yourself if the researchers of that disease are ignoring something that your team have already been analysing with great results.

Make a new educational system for Africa with lower costs and better results that could create opportunity for millions of people.

The money is out there for everyone, but only a few see it and want to take it.

Consider the options that are presented to you, keep in mind your knowledge, your contacts and the current market situation, and go for it.

24. DEVELOP YOUR OWN BUSINESS IDEA

You start to see business opportunities anywhere, but your focus on one winning idea and ability to discard others will be a key part of your success.

A great idea will be any that can solve an existing problem in the market, which you may have experienced yourself – for instance, as a user browsing a website: could you develop a website that will help users to find what they are looking for easier or in a better way? Or as a traveller: travelling by train when the ticket inspector *has* asked you for the ticket – wouldn't it be easier if the train itself already knew who paid with smart sensors?

Write down on paper or digitally all the ideas that come to mind, no matter how crazy you think they are today, and draw sketches, take photos, record audio, notes and any other element that will help you in the future to understand what you were thinking on this day. Then go and review that folder every now and then. Over the years, the world will invent new materials, processes, software and technology, so what seems unfeasible today will likely be in the market one day, so it's up to you to decide if you want to be the one making the income or have someone else get in front of you with developing that idea. So be aware of how everything evolves.

From my own list of ideas, there are already two in the market created from two different start-ups that are not mine, perfectly developed and doing what I already thought. Great – although unfortunately, I had no choice but to buy their products and congratulate them.

When an idea is winning the pulse in your head and you really think it can work, go to and analyse your chances of success by asking yourself:

What is the size of your market or industry? Can it be acquired only by a certain group of people from a specific location, or could it be of worldwide use?

Who are the competitors, and what are their business dynamics when it comes to expanding their market? A lot of competition predicts that the battle will be tough and you will have to sacrifice your margins, although no competition can indicate that other companies have tried and failed. If something is so innovative that even your future customers don't know they need it, you will have invested in educating the public and creating that demand for your product, through advertising and word of mouth.

How much would your customers pay for those services or products? And obviously, what costs would that mean for you in order to offer them? If your numbers don't work out positive, maybe it's not the right time to start, or the right product, unless you have a longer-term strategy and you can afford the risk to start with losses.

Google offers great free tools to take the first steps in your analysis: Google Trends and Google Ad Preview. With the former, you can see what trends are over time according to the volume of searches for certain keywords on Google, indicating if there is a growing interest and it makes sense to enter the market as soon as possible. And, with the latter, you will be able to visualize which results and companies appear in Google when searching and in what area of the world your clients may be located.

When all the signs point to success, just one more question: Do you assume that you might be completely wrong and that the execution of your idea may fail? Great, then go for it!

The phases of business creation will depend on the idea. Maybe you just have to develop a new website and position it well on Google, so my previous book *Visibility Online* could help you. Maybe you need external investments to make a new product that doesn't exist yet and market it, so finding manufacturers (e.g. Alibaba) and investors (e.g. crowdfunding platforms like Indiegogo) may be your first step.

Manage risk, create a brand and scale it gradually at a pace that allows you to maintain control, hiring more professionals and always maintaining the mission and vision of your initial idea.

25. OR INVEST IN SOMEONE ELSE'S IDEAS

If you are not one of those who is willing to stop sleeping peacefully to create a new company, you can always help those who are, and get a part of their cake if they succeed. Also known as being a business angel, but at a scale you can handle.

Every day there are thousands of entrepreneurs looking for resources, skills from others, marketing help, investment for product development, and in most cases, emotional support to push them forward.

Because you're not part of a recognized investment brand, entrepreneurs won't find you easily, but they are easy to be found: check out crowdfunding portals such as Indiegogo or Kickstarter, where every day there are many entrepreneurs promoting their projects and looking for small investments from the public to be able to progress. If you see that one is particularly good and you would like to help them more actively, contact them.

Other portals such as Freelancer, 99designs or Fiverr serve to help entrepreneurs to get in touch with someone with a particular skill they lack and it is the perfect place where you have to be attentive and detect a possible new big thing that will break the market.

There, you can find them asking for a web design for a new Ecommerce platform, for the cover of a new book, lines of code for the development of a new app, the design of an architecture project for a new restaurant in your city, and a thousand other opportunities.

Connect with those restless minds and learn more about their product, show your interest and find out how you can help.

What do you want in exchange? They will ask you this. So you will take part of the risk if their idea fails, but keep a percentage of the profit if it is successful.

For example, there are entrepreneurs designing a new jacket with a new fabric, ingenious games, a revolutionary video game controller that might be bought by PlayStation, the development of a new material for 3D printers with special features ... among many other ideas. Find them, contact them through these pages or their own websites, and propose to them that you could become their biggest investor in exchange for a percentage over the next 20 years if the product is successfully marketed.

Don't forget to delegate any legal issues and drafting contracts to your lawyer.

Each day is filled with new opportunities in which to invest your money to generate more passively. In addition, you can start with small investments, safer projects, learn from experience and scale up to create a powerful portfolio of new companies with great potential.

26. BUY LOW, SELL HIGH

This is the advice my parents should have repeated to me over and over again instead of eating vegetables.

If you want to acquire wealth, you need high margins, both to cover your costs and to obtain profits. The selling price of goods is defined by the market – either by what the buyers are willing to pay for something or because of the supply and demand principle, and it will also be mirrored by competitors selling the same goods.

So, open your eyes to see more clearly those occasions in which you can increase your margins in whatever you trade with. You have to detect opportunities in the market that others don't see. The trick is to be patient and manage the timing intelligently.

If you sell products, look for materials or products of a higher quality at a lower price beyond your geographical area of comfort. You will probably end up on alibaba.com or creating other international relations.

China is known for its low cost in production and manufacturing, but that doesn't mean that its quality is low. In fact, you would be surprised to know that more than 80% of the products we consume in Europe and the US are manufactured there.

If you want to invest in properties, do not rush, but establish very specific criteria in your searches to receive alerts of only those that are below the market price, where the square footage is considerably cheaper than the average and without getting distracted by the houses that everybody else is looking at, which happen to look nicer or are very central.

When you buy something that many others already have interest in, it's when it's already too late.

Buy when the demand is low, wait or create the interest yourself by renovating the house, and then sell.

If you invest in the stock exchange or Forex (currency trading), avoid any purchase at the current market price and put lower purchase limits to only acquire when the price falls. With this rule, you are more likely to get a profit sooner and be able to sell higher after a shorter time, rather than buying at a stock's peak.

I have repeated the concept several times, right? Well, I hope it has stayed with you, so don't buy again in a hurry, thinking that you are missing this opportunity that everyone talks about. Remember to avoid FOMO: fear of missing out.

27. GET READY TO ENTREPRENEUR

Entrepreneurship is not merely an activity but a way of life, a mentality governing the continuous search for how to make things better or create new products or services.

It's applicable both to the personal sphere (where you always think of new ways of doing the things you usually do), to the workplace of a company (improving processes and gaining efficiency in the team or in certain tasks), or for what it is most commonly known for, starting a business from a new idea.

Create a business model with a vision and a mission: to decide why it exists. Create a business that is bigger than yourself – that means not thinking as a freelancer. The main reason for this is because otherwise you can't scale your economic model. You should plan to employ more people, generate more products or services, serve more customers, and generate more income.

When you get that scalable model and generate income, don't forget to add to the recipe a system that replaces yourself too, so you don't have to be looped in on it while you continue generating money, while walking with your partner, travelling, playing with your children or sleeping. Do you remember about passive income? We want a company that enriches us, not a job.

When undertaking a business, control the risk and increment it gradually. Discuss the idea with friends and family, who will ideally have questions that will challenge you and help you improve your proposal. Do not worry if they laugh or mock you. That is the best part: think about how they will stop laughing when they see you succeed.

Undoubtedly, you will have to get involved in many parts of the business, from being the main sales rep interested in bringing new customers, establishing the accounting system that your team will use, and even to being the one looking for subsidies and news that affects your business. Try to delegate responsibilities and automate processes as much as you can. Often, it's convenient to invest in good software that will avoid your team spending hours drawing graphs or tables manually.

Try not to borrow too much and do not rush prematurely. Do not plan to be rich in a few months, because you will overwhelm yourself with goals that nobody apart from you has set up. Actually, it's more likely you'll have losses than profit during the first months or years.

Remember always to pay yourself and plan your vacation at the beginning of the year, or run the risk of becoming a slave to your own idea.

Prepare to fail many times, and start over with the same or more energy in each new attempt. Success will come with patience and continuous effort.

28. MANAGE SUCCESS WITH SUCCESS

It's as important to get ready to win as it is to be prepared for when you are winning. Remember that success is not a destination, but the whole path of achievements and progress, and you must enjoy it in each of its moments with satisfaction and fulfilment.

Enjoy and celebrate every time you step up, reaching towards that higher happiness and personal fulfilment you are looking for – which is different for everyone.

Show respect, always. People adore winners who are polite, attentive, generous and kind, and hate the arrogant and narcissistic ones.

Stories of those lonely rich people are not fiction. Unfortunately – and even more in those who achieved success in a very short time and effortlessly – they forget their values and treat others with arrogance and contempt, and there will come a time when money will not allow them to buy love or friendship, and it will begin their end and their misery. They will stop winning.

Others invest so much in order to get where they are that they are trapped like mice running on a wheel, in which they do nothing but run and spin, thinking of nothing else than being in the office and sleeping. And remember that, as I once read in the prologue of a book, "Nobody on his deathbed ever regretted not having spent more hours in the office."

If you are one of those whose success is measured in social recognition, as a public figure with a high number of followers, then how you handle your success will be determined not only by how you behave in your private relationships, but also in public ones. Assume that you are who you are because of your followers, so give them back the love they give you, which is now easier than ever with social networks. Answer the messages, let yourself take pictures, interact with your audience and not only when there is a brand advantage or an economic return. Be grateful.

Use your wealth and success to make those around you live better. Never forget your loved ones, friends and even strangers who are in worse conditions than you and for whom you can do something to make them feel better.

Remember that thing about adding value to humanity during your time here.

29. WORK ON YOUR RESUME (CV) CONSTANTLY

There are those who go to the doctor when they get sick and those who take care of themselves to avoid going to the doctor.

There are those who prepare their curriculum vitae when they need to find a new job and those who work on their CV while they have a job, so they do not have to look at it again.

When you stand out, both in your company and in your personal life, you may never need to do an interview again, because either your company will never let you go or other companies will be offering you new opportunities.

It's great you have a job now, but what will happen if you get fired or encounter an unsustainable working relationship with someone in your workplace, and you decide that the best thing is to move out of your company? Most likely, you will go and search for your resume in some lost folders on your computer, update the information and date of your last role, and only then are you ready to go.

Imagine if you had worked on your CV during this time, and now you can add, in addition to your latest responsibilities in your company, some successful case studies and achievements you have under your belt, a new language, or a new technical skill that you were learning, or that business training or new discipline you signed up for out of working hours.

Aside from all that, imagine that all this information is already perfectly updated on your LinkedIn profile in several languages, along with some recommendations for each of the positions in which you have worked.

Once you increase, update and maintain your value, it will be normal for other companies to identify you as a talent they are after and approach you, but in any case you should always be keeping an eye open for offers out there getting advertised.

Create alerts on LinkedIn and on the main job sites to send you an email when they detect new potential opportunities for you as your next step.

By studying job offers, you will also keep abreast of the skills required in the companies you would like to work in, in addition to the years of experience they require. Do they usually ask for languages, certain skills, case studies of leadership or demonstrable experience of you being a great seller?

Here and now is when you have time to get ready for that desired position, not when you lose your current job.

Improve day by day to compete for that opportunity tomorrow.

IV. HAVE A PROFESSIONAL CAREER WITHOUT LIMITS

30. SET OFF IN A NEW COMPANY ON THE RIGHT FOOT

Getting promoted to a new position is always a sweet challenge, but even more so if it's in a new company. It's crucial to keep some tips in mind to establish those social and professional links that will make you succeed.

You may have already had the opportunity to meet your team before you start. It depends on the culture of the company, but to have a drink and a relaxed chat with them can be very helpful for a new member of staff who is just starting.

It's important to adjust your expectations about the company and what it can do for your professional career. Take some time to understand its culture and structure, and show the correct attitude during the adaptation process. Try to build a solid and positive internal reputation, avoiding mistakes during the first months and increasing your confidence over time.

Understand why they hired you and don't lose sight of that that, because it will determine your success. Set aside large, difficult, and important decisions for the near future, and do not rush them.

Ask for help and question everything. In this early period, you're buying time to allow you to analyse your co-workers and bosses and to sketch a first impression of them, as they are doing for you too.

Therefore, be respectful and pretend to be shy. A person who is intelligent, thoughtful, and subtle will get along with both the introverts and extroverts of your team, but if you go in with large extroversion and make a lot of noise, you will split your audience very soon: introverts may feel threatened because of your perceived sense of superiority, while extroverts may see you as a competitor (socially as well as professionally).

Open your eyes and shut your mouth. Take notes on everything you see that you could improve, but do not try to change things right away. Learn first the politics of your company, which you will need to understand in order to change them. Think about this: Why were they not changed before and who could be impacted negatively because of that?

In time you will shine in your new company, but consider it a planned and staged brightness, so that your colleagues have a chance to put on their sunglasses. And while there's nothing wrong with trying to shine, remember that you can also focus on making those around you look good rather than yourself. By being a team player, you may end up dazzling far more than if you are a soloist.

31. ENJOY DOING IT OR DON'T DO IT AT ALL

If, every morning, you get up to go to work for the simple fact of getting a salary, then in the evenings you spend hours watching TV, and on the weekend you do things that are on your to-do list but are more for commitment than pleasure... then it's going to be hard for you to be happy and shine as a person.

You may be lacking a passion and something to focus on in which you devote a good amount of energy, where the hours fly by and, if you can, get paid for it. You will stand out when you do things that motivate you, have fun doing them and, at the same time, you monetize that activity.

Becoming the best in something means performing much better than the rest do, dedicating many more hours than a simple workday and you may even have to invest many other resources in it, so make sure it's something you enjoy doing.

Forget what some losers say about not turning a hobby into a job. They spend 10 hours in the office miserably to enjoy their hobby once a month. You can work on your passion and hobby for five hours a day, make more money, and when you get bored of it, then evolve and adapt your profession to the next hobby.

Do you need a little more clarity? Imagine being a ski instructor because you love skiing, creating a bar/restaurant in which all sports are televised because you're a fan, or playing old movies, setting up a kindergarten, a pet reception center, becoming a tour guide for your city ... or opening a tourist center in each city, for which you will have to travel a lot, know places, understand their culture, hire local employees and, once assembled, go to the next city that you and your family would like to visit.

Analyse your hobbies, who you enjoy doing them with, and which company you spend money with when you do them. Now think of a plan to work in that company or create a better one.

You need to find your passion as soon as possible and charge for working on it. It does not matter if your market is small – the more specific it is, the easier it will be for you to create a strong reputation. There are many who like the same as you.

32. GIVE 120%, ALWAYS

Here's a story: I was having dinner at a Michelin two-star restaurant in London and had the opportunity to meet and talk with the chef at the end of the dinner, who, with great kindness, came out from the kitchen, commented on the dishes we ate and explained a little about the history of the restaurant.

I asked her, what does a restaurant have to do to get two Michelin stars?

She replied: "Give 120% to each client. From when they enter the restaurant until they leave. Give to everyone the best experience we can, because, truthfully, anyone could be a judge of the Michelin guide, including you guys."

That made me see that excellence is achieved by being excellent, always and with everyone. Convert that high level of professionalism as your new standard.

Now you: go back to your job, give 120% in your day today. When you work on a project, with clients, with your bosses or your team, don't forget to give the best version of yourself on each occasion for this simple reason: anyone could influence your promotion in the company, or any client could bring you more work in the future, and recommend you to other potential clients.

Think, what else can you offer in addition to what they have requested you? What would amaze you from someone if you requested them the same thing?

The best are those who always give their best. Those who outperform the rest. Those whom the bosses remember when a new position has been created.

If you have a business and sell products or services, focus your efforts on adding more value to what you do regularly and differ from the competition.

If you are a teacher, you have the possibility to shape the thoughts and actions of many children and your responsibility is very high. Leave your problems at home and give your best in each class.

If you are a public administrator, you don't have to be satisfied with giving the minimum in a job that is secure for life, simply because others do that. You work for citizens and you represent a large community. Stand out and create great value for the people.

The same goes for the managers, masons, lawyers, waiters, businessmen or policemen. Think about your trade and imagine what the best professional would be like in your position, with your clients, with your colleagues and with the company.

Become 'them' today.

33. PRESENT TO IMPRESS

Presenting to your team, the whole company or to a client is a fantastic opportunity to shine. Trust in yourself, make the most of it and don't be afraid. If it's you who is presenting, it's because someone considered that you were the best to share that message, and from that instant, you're already playing with the advantage of wearing the label of 'expert'.

To deliver a great presentation is not luck, but training. Practise at home several times till you flow, record yourself with your laptop or phone, watch the recording and identify mistakes that you should correct, like your body language or voiceover.

Go to the meeting room with plenty of time before everyone arrives to make sure that any technical element works as expected: the projector, the sound if you play video, the light in the room, how the colours of the text are projected and whether they are easy to read on the background, how much space you have for moving around and what volume of voice you have to talk with to reach the last row.

If it's a meeting sitting around a table with specific attendees, try to decide beforehand where you will sit to have the decision maker in front of you. Hide the spare chairs in a corner or different room and place the ones that are going to be used strategically around the table. If you expect people who don't know each other, you could use labels with their names standing on the table because, in addition to helping them get to know each other, you will guide them to where you want them to sit.

When presenting, don't move too much, don't speak looking at the screen or slides, but look into the eyes of the audience. Control the movement of your hands and body and use them to enhance your speech.

Structure your content very well with a clear goal in mind of what you want to achieve, and don't forget to conclude and define the next steps with specific deadlines.

The use of slides is not mandatory. The best speakers are those who don't need visual support or who are drawing on a whiteboard, but if you use PowerPoint or similar, then make sure you tell the story with as few slides as possible and avoid distractions with animations or transitions.

Check the format of each slide that is going to be shown, test the sound of the video if there is one, and use these to help navigate through the presentation. Using a good table of contents and showing it before each section can help a lot so that your audience doesn't get lost.

Constantly read the audience in front of you. If they're looking at their computers or phones it's a clear message that you are losing their attention and, in addition to knowing that you have to put more emphasis on the way you're telling the story, you can also ask some questions to see how they interact with you and whether they look back at you again. But, be careful – don't ask those who were obviously not listening, because you may embarrass them and lose any business opportunity you had with that presentation.

34. INTERVIEW AND HIRE TALENT

One of the best investments you will make in your hours of work will be to create a winning team around you who take care of your success, the success of the company, of their colleagues and of your clients.

Because of this, the recruitment process has to be taken very seriously and go to get the best talent that exists out there, in skills, experience and ability. This will take you more time and money than hiring an employee who is just 'not bad'. As the subtitle of the book says, being 'good' is no longer good enough.

When interviewing a candidate, it's also very important you promote your company, team and day-to-day work in the same way that candidates have to promote themselves. Many only evaluate with lots of questions and forget that candidates with great talent have more offers and the possibility to choose from several opportunities.

Start the interview by explaining about your company, the team the candidate could be working with and, more importantly, the position they applied for. This explanation will help them to relax, adapt their conversational tone to yours and if they are smart, they will adapt their future responses to the context you just described.

Once you move to question time, adapt your questions subtly to make sure you really get an answer for what you are looking for. For example, if you need a leader for your team, focus your questions on personnel management, challenges they had with employees, how many of their previous team would follow them to the new company, how you motivated them at low times, or how you protected them in stressful situations.

Finally, don't forget to surprise them with some unexpected and random questions that will put the candidate in an unguarded position, which will help you analyse that person in a more subjective way and how they can fit with other employees. For instance, what is left for them to do in this life? How would their perfect Sunday be if everything were possible?

Create a recruitment process for all those who apply to join your team, and because you can't interview every candidate, you will have to train junior staff for them to learn to interview with practice and to enjoy the new responsibility – it's even great for them to have a chemistry session with their future co-workers.

Those team members will analyse and filter the majority of the candidates, moving to the next round only those who have passed certain skills required on a day-to-day basis, like technical ones, commercial, written, creative, or simply professional communication skills, among others.

Turn each of your team into a talent scout.

35. LEAD TEAMS

Using your team as resources you have at your disposal for eight hours a day in exchange for their salary will not take you very far in your career.

Nobody likes to work for a bad boss and, sooner or later, they will start coming to work demotivated and you will get the minimum delivery from them, and they will think of resigning, in addition to providing a guaranteed miserable environment.

Leaders do not have helpers, but an army of people with ambition who are willing to work hard for a greater good than themselves.

Become a leader for your team, transmitting your passion and ambition for the work you do. Help them to progress and dedicate time to each of them individually, so they have time and space to talk about what they want.

Try to know them at a level beyond the professional, so, if you organize team activities such as a dinner, suggest that they come with their partners or family members.

Do not limit yourself to asking them for things you need at that moment, or telling them how to do it and when. Instead, let them be part of the medium and long-term vision and understanding of why you are doing it, and what you want to achieve.

They may surprise you with a new idea or delivery of something that is much better than what you expected, or it could be done more efficiently, in a way that you didn't even think of.

Spend time training them, explaining processes, products, customers and the business model of your company.

Get them to work hard during the day, but encourage them to go home on time and relax, distract themselves and come back stronger and fresher the next day.

Be demanding to get the best out of them, and reward their efforts with the right gratitude so that they feel the appreciation of the company but in a way you can sustain it in the future.

Give them constant feedback on their performance and worry about their development and progression. Also, ask them to give feedback to you for your own improvement. One easy and comfortable way to ask for feedback is to say: "Every other week I will ask you for one thing that I or we could do better as a team". In this way, if, during this period of time, something happened and they disagreed with you completely or thought that it could have been done in another way, they now know that they will have the opportunity to comment on it at your next meeting.

Finally always remember this as a leader: when something goes wrong, take the blame and take responsibility to protect the team. And if it goes well, it's because of their effort, so give them credit.

36. ADD VALUE TO ANY MEETING

We all have many meetings during the day which mostly are only remembered when our agenda notifies us 15 minutes before they start. We go and we hope that someone will take the lead. Yes, even those leaders that are supposed to be leading.

Prepare your week or your day with enough anticipation. Reject calendar invites for those meetings that you don't need to be at or where it's likely you won't contribute at all. However, for those meetings that you are planning to attend, make the most of it: find out who is also attending, propose a potential agenda to the participants if it doesn't yet exist and invite them to add more points if needed.

Make sure that the invite contains all the necessary technical details for the participants, such as the conference telephone numbers for each person who will dial in, and ensure that presentations or spreadsheets which will be discussed are attached, and the video conference works and you can share the screen with the others if necessary. Do you see how you are already standing out and the meeting has not started yet?

During the meeting, take notes, let others speak, wait for your turn and, when your opportunity comes, expose your points and make yourself heard. If you think that the conversation falls on a tangent that diverts the attention and interests of the audience, be the one that interrupts and leads the conversation back to today's goal. Suggest that this other conversation could be discussed at another time and with the right group.

Depending on the set up of the debate, get up and write the agreed conclusions or action points on a whiteboard or large sheet of paper.

After the meeting, write those notes in an email with the points discussed and the next steps, with their owners and the deadlines needed to execute them. You can send it after a few hours or even days (so in that way, you will refresh the conversation when it seems forgotten).

The leader is not made by a title, but because they execute leadership. Any opportunity is good to demonstrate your proactivity and initiative.

37. PROMOTE IN YOUR COMPANY

There always will be a few co-workers who indulge in most of the gossip, who speak badly about the company, or about the bosses, and probably about you when you're not there. They are the ones we all met at school, who wanted to be the popular ones and others wanted to follow them to feel socially united.

But forget about the playground. This is business.

Those who progress in a company are those who understand a very simple concept: Make your bosses succeed. Understand what their ambitions are and what they need to get there.

Help them with the research, with the presentation, speaking well about them, encouraging them, and being genuinely interested in how everything is going. If you still don't understand this idea completely, imagine for a second that you are the boss: wouldn't you prefer your team to be actively helping you to succeed instead of putting up barriers and complaining? And who would you promote given the moment – the person who complains or the person who is involved? Simple.

If you don't know how your success is going to be evaluated at the end of the year, ask them as soon as you have a chance. Is it according to the number of new clients that you bring, generating more sales, improving the productivity or efficiency of the team, punctuality in delivery of results, or net profit?

Find out and start working on this. Soon you will become indispensable and your progression will have no limits. You will not do an interview again.

If you work with clients, then your company, your bosses, and you will be successful if you do the same with them: What does it take to make your clients succeed?

If you are a bar's beverage supplier, don't just try to think of how to sell more drinks to the bar, but think how that bar can sell more to its customers. Tell them about some good ideas that you saw in other bars that could also work in theirs, like installing WIFI or televising soccer games if they do not have those services yet. Or even, respectfully, advising them of things that they should improve in the bar to attract more customers, regardless of whether they drink your brand or not, such as adding an additional waiter to reduce waiting time from customers, or keeping the bathrooms clean during the course of the day. They will see you as a partner and will trust you more, not seeing you just as a drinks provider who wants to sell them as much as possible.

Become a personalized case study and prepare your conversations about your promotion when the time arrives, in a solid and structured way, listing everything you have achieved both on your own and with your boss, and the value you have added.

Become excellent and indispensable, and make clear how foolish it would be for a company to let you go.

38. DISMISS IF NECESSARY

If you have been in charge of a team, you will know that there are times that you have been supervising certain workers who perform below average.

Perhaps because of their limited capacity or, normally, because of their attitude. They do not have the same passion or responsibility as the rest, and it goes without saying that they might have acted unprofessionally in a project, with a client or a co-worker.

Dismiss them. The road is very long, the horse gets tired and we cannot afford to carry unnecessary weight.

Companies value a good leader not just for making successes happen, but also for eliminating the blockages that lead us to them.

If their behaviour has been constantly below the expected level, a warning or dismissal should not be a surprise to them, so perform regular reviews where you give feedback and listen to what they want to say – that's very important as well.

In some of these catch-ups, try to bring a third person in the room, preferably human resources, because if you are alone there is the risk they will take things out of context or misinterpret your message and use it against you.

Before firing someone, make sure that human resources is aligned with you and they explain to you how the process needs to be done correctly, as the company wants to avoid complaints or litigations for unfair dismissal.

On the day of dismissal, if possible, send the person home directly from the meeting room without having access to their computer again. IT will need to cancel their emails so they lose connectivity from every device, adding an automatic reply, informing that they no longer work in the company and someone else should be contacted now.

A softer way to fire someone is to 'invite' them to leave, limiting their progression in the company based on objectives that won't be achieved, so no promotion or pay rise will be possible. However, if they are people with no ambition and these risks won't matter to them, they might become a liability enough so that you have no other option than to accompany them to the door.

Only when you feel that you are the worst on your team, do you have the right team.

39. COMPETE AND THRIVE

When you begin to stand out, two things will happen: some will envy you and slowly move away from your path since this route is not suitable for them, and others will feel challenged and will want to improve themselves by entering into healthy competition with you.

Maybe at the beginning it will bother you that a friend starts to develop an idea which has come from yours, or that a process in your team producing high results is copied by another team leader, or even by other companies. But later, you will realize that you inspired them to do what they do (yes, it is your accomplishment that they are progressing), and at the same time they are stimulating you to improve your current work further, or to perfect your next project.

Create competitiveness in your team, either against another team in the same company, or among your team members. It rewards those who try harder and go further, as long as they don't damage the integrity of the team as such.

The best way to thank them for their efforts is usually with public recognition, that their name reaches someone higher in the company and helps their internal reputation.

If their success was due to a specific task, then reward them. Something material can work, such as two tickets to a musical, or dinner with their partner.

So, do not be afraid to share your discoveries, your results or the results of your team, which make you stand out from the rest. Remember, however competitive you become, always act with respect and modesty towards others, as there may be a fine line between them admiring or hating you.

CONCLUSION: YOU CAN

SHINE helps you to visualize what a successful person is like and how they behave, are loved and are able to enjoy the best things around them.

There are no losers, no mediocracy or people with no value, and any of us has room for improvement – there are only those who want to improve and those who do not. If you convert any of these 39 tips into a habit, you have already taken a huge step forward for the continuous improvement of your persona and thanks to the simplicity of the book and its structure, you can reread it several times a year to remind you of some important points that you forgot, or of others that didn't really apply to you at the time, but now, because your personal circumstances have changed, can be read in a different way.

You just have to get started with a small win, take one step up, and inertia will do the rest.

The positive chemistry of your body will transmit security and well-being to others, making them want to approach you. Your acquiring power will attract more capital and solve many of your problems, and over time, you will get powerful new connections with excellent people with whom you will want to change the world as much as possible.

Remember, you exist to add value to humanity and to those who come after you to continue making progress with your achievements. Shine!

THANK YOU

How many times have you felt alluded to while reading this book, and have you stopped to think that you should apply some of this advice in your day-to-day, with your family, with your personal finances or in your company? Great. Now is the time to execute and transform this ambition into results, to improve year by year in every aspect of your life. It's time for you to shine and to give light to those who accompany you on this journey and, at the same time, lengthen the shadow of those behind you.

Give a copy of this book to your friends, family, employees or to your team. To those whose potential you fully trust.

Share your stories with me at the following email address, or leave a review of this book on Amazon to help others to find it and get inspired.

Email: info@bernatriera.es

www.ingramcontent.com/pod-product-compliance
Lightning Source LLC
Chambersburg PA
CBHW022043190326
41520CB00008B/686